# Complete Graded Spelling Lists for Years One to Six

## AMERICAN ENGLISH

KIT'S EDUCATIONAL PUBLISHING

ISBN-13: 978-1495455308
ISBN-10: 1495455300

:

# CONTENTS

# INTRODUCTION

Speaking a language is an ability that is learned naturally by children living in society. Writing a language, by contrast, requires determined effort. It does not come naturally, even to those who are surrounded by the written word. It must be actively taught and learned by means of an extended and repetitive process of trial and error. This is particularly so in the case of English, where so many words break the spelling conventions, such as they are.

The ability to spell is clearly central to the ability to write a language; it is no less central to the ability to read. The art of reading effortlessly and with enjoyment is closely correlated with the ability to identify a written word quickly and accurately. Once again, this is particularly difficult in English, because of its unruly spelling. It is thus a great advantage, both to a child's writing and to his or her reading, to have acquired the art of spelling.

As with anything that must be learned by trial and error, it helps to have resources to make the learning process systematic. This book is intended as such a resource. It is intended primarily for use by parents and teachers as a basic tool in the teaching and testing of spelling to a child. It may also be helpful those learning English later in life and/or as a second language.

The words are ordered in spelling groups, so as to reinforce the spelling rule by way of repetition. The groups follow the developmental stages of learning, from the simple short and long vowel sounds (*pan, pane*), through blended and doubled consonants (*brand, barrow*), unstressed syllables and irregular phonetic rules (mir*ror*, monol*ogue*) and on to compounded prefixes and suffixes (*appropriate, representation*). The spelling follows that of the *Merriam-Webster's Collegiate Dictionary*.

The ordering principle for the words within a list is generally alphabetic, using the first and/or last letters of the word and/or the word's primary phonetic element. The many exceptions to this principle are made to accommodate words that vary from standard phonetic rules and patterns. Exceptions are also introduced to add variety, for those who are following the lists in the order given.

The extra words in each week are either less common words which follow the same spelling pattern or words which build on the listed words, principally by the addition of prefixes and/or suffixes. These extra words thus help to teach further spelling rules and show how words within a word family are related (*festive/festival /festivity*, etc.).

The advantage of having a complete set of spelling lists for the elementary school  years is that one can pursue the program as best suits the abilities and interests of the child. Children's aptitudes vary greatly in this area as in others: some take to spelling very easily, while others find they need to concentrate on it more intensively to acquire the basic skills. This book provides one list per week for six years - with two weeks off per year! - but can be pursued at the level and pace that suits your child.

The best advice that can be given to those with little experience of teaching spelling is that the process is most successful when it is interactive. If you are a parent using these lists to teach and test your child's spelling, try to find ways to personalize your teaching and to make it fun. For example, ask your child to make up silly sentences to include as many words on a spelling list as possible. Your child will be more likely to remember how to spell a word if he or she has made up his or her own rule for learning it. The books of exercises in this series follow the same lists and so may be used to aid your learning program.

# YEAR 1

| YEAR 1    LIST 1 | YEAR 1    LIST 2 |
|---|---|
| bat | yes |
| cat | bet |
| fat | get |
| hat | let |
| mat | met |
| pat | set |
| rat | big |
| sat | dig |
| bib | pig |
| nib | wig |
| rib | bit |
| bin | fit |
| fin | hit |
| pin | lit |
| tin | pit |
| win | sit |

| EXTRA WORDS | EXTRA WORDS |
|---|---|
| vat | jet |
| fib | fig |
| pats | kit |
| ribs | pigs |
| wins | fits |

## YEAR 1   LIST 3

ban
can
fan
man
pan
ran
van
net
pet
vet
wet
yet
hop
mop
pop
top

## YEAR 1   LIST 4

dam
ham
jam
ram
cap
gap
lap
map
nap
sap
tap
tax
wax
his
fix
mix

## EXTRA WORDS

tan
lop
vans
gets
mops

## EXTRA WORDS

rap
maps
waxes
fixes
mixes

| YEAR 1   LIST 5 | YEAR 1   LIST 6 |
|---|---|
| bug | am |
| dug | an |
| hug | as |
| jug | at |
| mug | add |
| rug | all |
| bid | and |
| did | are |
| hid | arm |
| kid | art |
| lid | ago |
| rid | bar |
| bun | car |
| fun | far |
| run | jar |
| sun | tar |

| EXTRA WORDS | EXTRA WORDS |
|---|---|
| lug | ax |
| tug | ark |
| gun | adding |
| nun | barring |
| pun | jarring |

## YEAR 1    LIST 7

bag
nag
rag
sag
tag
wag
bob
cob
job
mob
rob
sob
bud
mud
suds
bus

## YEAR 1    LIST 8

bed
fed
led
red
wed
beg
leg
peg
cot
dot
got
hot
lot
not
pot
rot

## EXTRA WORDS

gag
lag
buses
sagged
bobbed

## EXTRA WORDS

keg
jot
dotted
wedding
begging

## YEAR 1    LIST 13

if
in
is
it
die
lie
pie
tie
hi
ill
inn
up
us
due
for
nor

## YEAR 1    LIST 14

of
off
on
or
ox
go
no
so
do
to
too
zoo
does
goes
son
won

### EXTRA WORDS

lies
pies
ties
dying
lying

### EXTRA WORDS

into
onto
upon
doing
going

## YEAR 1    LIST 15

deed
feed
need
reed
seed
weed
doom
room
loom
moon
noon
soon
boot
hoot
loot
root

## YEAR 1    LIST 16

seem
deep
keep
peep
seep
weep
feet
meet
food
mood
coop
hoop
loop
good
hood
wood

### EXTRA WORDS

heed
toot
needed
doomed
booted

### EXTRA WORDS

deem
teem
seemed
looped
wooded

| YEAR 1   LIST 17 | YEAR 1   LIST 18 |
|---|---|
| card | beef |
| hard | reef |
| yard | leek |
| bark | meek |
| dark | peek |
| mark | seek |
| park | week |
| farm | feel |
| harm | heel |
| warm | peel |
| barn | reel |
| yarn | book |
| cart | cook |
| dart | hook |
| part | look |
| tart | took |

| EXTRA WORDS | EXTRA WORDS |
|---|---|
| lard | reek |
| lark | keel |
| kart | nook |
| harder | feeling |
| darker | cooking |

## YEAR 1    LIST 19

been
keen
seen
deer
jeer
peer
veer
cool
fool
pool
tool
wool
hoof
roof
door
poor

## YEAR 1    LIST 20

you
your
our
out
any
many
put
has
was
said
this
that
have
give
live
love

## EXTRA WORDS

moor
fooled
peered
woolly
poorly

## EXTRA WORDS

outing
giving
living
loving
putting

## YEAR 1     LIST 21

back
pack
rack
sack
deck
neck
peck
kick
lick
pick
sick
tick
wick
dock
lock
sock

## YEAR 1     LIST 22

mock
rock
buck
duck
luck
suck
tuck
less
mess
kiss
miss
boss
loss
moss
toss
fuss

### EXTRA WORDS

tack
nick
cock
packing
ticking

### EXTRA WORDS

muck
hiss
lucky
messy
fussy

| YEAR 1    LIST 23 | YEAR 1    LIST 24 |
|---|---|
| ball | bill |
| call | fill |
| fall | gill |
| hall | hill |
| mall | kill |
| tall | mill |
| wall | pill |
| bell | sill |
| fell | will |
| sell | dull |
| tell | gull |
| well | bull |
| yell | full |
| doll | pull |
| roll | cuff |
| toll | puff |

| EXTRA WORDS | EXTRA WORDS |
|---|---|
| pall | cull |
| dell | hull |
| loll | lull |
| poll | huff |
| tolled | muff |

| YEAR 1    LIST 25 | YEAR 1    LIST 26 |
|---|---|
| chap | ash |
| chat | cash |
| chin | dash |
| chip | lash |
| chop | sash |
| chug | dish |
| rich | fish |
| much | wish |
| such | bush |
| she | push |
| shy | shoe |
| shed | shut |
| shin | shall |
| ship | shell |
| shop | shook |
| shot | shoot |

| EXTRA WORDS | EXTRA WORDS |
|---|---|
| chum | gash |
| sham | mash |
| shun | gosh |
| chugging | lashes |
| shopping | pushes |

## YEAR 1    LIST 27

quit
quiz
queen
queer
quack
quick
than
then
them
thin
thus
bath
path
with
both
moth

### EXTRA WORDS

thud
thug
thee
bathing
quizzing

## YEAR 1    LIST 28

sky
fly
spy
cry
dry
fry
try
bay
day
hay
lay
may
pay
ray
say
way

### EXTRA WORDS

cries
flies
spies
days
ways

## YEAR 1    LIST 29

boy
coy
joy
toy
dew
few
new
sew
jaw
law
paw
raw
saw
dawn
lawn
yawn

## YEAR 1    LIST 30

owe
own
bow
low
mow
row
tow
owl
bow
cow
how
now
row
gown
down
town

## EXTRA WORDS

pew
news
hawk
fawn
pawn

## EXTRA WORDS

sow
vow
wow
lower
rower

## YEAR 1    LIST 31

ant
pant
band
hand
land
sand
bank
dank
lank
rank
sank
tank
camp
damp
lamp
ramp

## YEAR 1    LIST 32

end
bend
lend
mend
send
tend
belt
felt
melt
best
nest
pest
rest
test
vest
west

### EXTRA WORDS

yank
rant
handy
sandy
tanker

### EXTRA WORDS

pelt
jest
zest
sender
tender

| YEAR 1    LIST 33 | YEAR 1    LIST 34 |
|---|---|
| king | old |
| ring | bold |
| sing | cold |
| wing | fold |
| ink | gold |
| link | hold |
| mink | sold |
| pink | told |
| sink | gong |
| wink | long |
| hint | song |
| mint | loft |
| risk | soft |
| fist | pomp |
| list | romp |
| mist | tongs |

| EXTRA WORDS | EXTRA WORDS |
|---|---|
| kink | colder |
| rink | folder |
| tint | longer |
| inky | olden |
| misty | golden |

## YEAR 1     LIST 35

fund
hung
lung
rung
sung
bulb
gulf
bulk
hulk
bunk
dunk
junk
sunk
gulp
pulp
hunt

## YEAR 1     LIST 36

crab
grab
glad
drag
flag
clam
slam
pram
tram
plan
clap
flap
slap
snap
trap
flat

### EXTRA WORDS

sulk
hunk
punt
runt
sunken

### EXTRA WORDS

brag
bran
clan
slammed
snapped

## YEAR 1    LIST 37

bled
fled
bred
stem
step
prod
frog
from
flop
crop
drop
stop
plot
slot
spot
trot

## YEAR 1    LIST 38

slid
twig
slim
skim
trim
swim
skin
spin
grin
twin
skip
clip
slip
drip
grip
trip

### EXTRA WORDS

sled
sped
clod
clog
blot

### EXTRA WORDS

skid
grid
brim
grim
prim

| YEAR 1   LIST 39 | YEAR 1   LIST 40 |
|---|---|
| crib | bake |
| flip | cake |
| snip | fake |
| spit | lake |
| grit | make |
| club | take |
| snub | wake |
| plug | base |
| slug | case |
| drum | vase |
| glum | bike |
| plum | hike |
| slum | like |
| swum | bite |
| spun | kite |
| stun | site |

| EXTRA WORDS | EXTRA WORDS |
|---|---|
| grub | rake |
| stub | sake |
| smug | mite |
| flit | alike |
| slit | awake |

## YEAR 1    LIST 41

ate
date
fate
gate
hate
late
mate
rate
ode
code
rode
home
dome
cope
hope
rope

## YEAR 1    LIST 41

fade
made
wade
came
fame
game
lame
name
same
tame
dine
fine
line
mine
pine
vine

### EXTRA WORDS

mode
lope
fateful
hateful
hopeful

### EXTRA WORDS

jade
dame
fading
saving
mining

## YEAR 1    LIST 43

ape
cape
gape
tape
cave
gave
pave
rave
save
wave
file
mile
pile
tile
dive
hive

## YEAR 1    LIST 44

safe
life
wife
cane
lane
mane
pane
sane
vane
rise
wise
hide
ride
side
tide
wide

### EXTRA WORDS

vile
nape
nave
diner
diver

### EXTRA WORDS

wane
rider
wider
wisely
safely

## YEAR 1    LIST 45

act
fact
pact
tact
bang
fang
gang
hang
rang
sang
tang
held
desk
help
yelp
left

### EXTRA WORDS

pang
weld
deft
helpful
tactful

## YEAR 1    LIST 46

bent
dent
lent
rent
sent
tent
went
helm
kept
wept
next
text
gift
lift
sift
film

### EXTRA WORDS

vent
rift
kiln
dented
lifted

| YEAR 1    LIST 47 | YEAR 1    LIST 48 |
|---|---|
| bond | limp |
| fond | hilt |
| pond | kilt |
| bolt | tilt |
| jolt | wilt |
| cost | milk |
| lost | silk |
| dusk | golf |
| husk | wolf |
| tusk | bump |
| bust | dump |
| dust | hump |
| gust | jump |
| just | lump |
| must | pump |
| rust | rump |

| EXTRA WORDS | EXTRA WORDS |
|---|---|
| musk | gilt |
| rusk | lilt |
| font | silt |
| fondly | silky |
| costly | jumpy |

| YEAR 1    LIST 49 | YEAR 1    LIST 50 |
|---|---|
| bale | pipe |
| gale | ripe |
| male | wipe |
| pale | lime |
| sale | mime |
| tale | time |
| joke | robe |
| poke | hole |
| woke | mole |
| dose | pole |
| hose | role |
| nose | sole |
| pose | bone |
| rose | cone |
| note | lone |
| vote | tone |

| EXTRA WORDS | EXTRA WORDS |
|---|---|
| dale | lobe |
| vale | dime |
| yoke | dole |
| dote | timing |
| woken | wiping |

# YEAR 1     REVISION LIST

| | | |
|---|---|---|
| rib | get | dig |
| fox | pod | mug |
| ago | far | sob |
| rag | lot | peg |
| dim | jam | egg |
| hat | bee | hut |
| gum | mop | ill |
| sun | mix | die |
| zoo | due | wood |
| keep | so | roof |
| yard | harm | took |
| live | put | neck |
| lock | reef | less |
| hoot | duck | fall |
| deer | full | soon |
| roll | chat | shop |
| hill | sash | quiz |
| thus | dry | ray |
| shoe | dew | dawn |
| own | gown | jaw |
| lamp | rank | quick |
| tow | pink | list |
| gong | soft | gulp |
| rose | fold | rest |
| slam | stem | felt |
| drum | vote | lake |
| swim | wish | vine |
| mile | game | glad |
| wave | bath | trip |
| kite | desk | help |
| gift | wept | queen |
| gust | bump | spot |
| wolf | mole | wipe |
| | rich | |

# YEAR 2

| | |
|---|---|
| Lists 1-2 | Common words |
| Lists 3-5 | Words with a long vowel sound |
| List 6 | Words starting with *wh-* |
| List 7 | Words starting with *th-*, words with soft *g* |
| List 8 | Words with a soft *c* |
| List 9 | Words ending in *-ss* |
| List 10 | Words ending in *-ff* or *-ll* |
| List 11 | Words with *ai* |
| List 12 | Words with *ai* or *oi* |
| List 13 | Words ending in *-y* or *-ye* |
| List 14 | Words with *ea* |
| List 15 | Words with *oa* |
| Lists 16-17 | Words ending in *-ck* |
| Lists 18-19 | Words with *ee* |
| List 20 | Words with *aw* or *ew* |
| List 21 | Words with *ow* |
| List 22 | Words with *ow* or *oo* |
| List 23 | Words with *oo* |
| Lists 24-28 | More words with a long vowel sound |
| Lists 29-30 | More words with a long vowel sound |
| List 31 | Words with *ir* or *or* |
| List 32 | Words with *or* |
| List 33 | Words with *ur* |
| List 34 | Words with *er* or *ou* |
| Lists 35-36 | More words with *ea* |
| Lists 37-37 | Words starting with *sh-* |
| List 39 | Words ending in *-sh* |
| List 40 | Words ending in *-sh* or *-th* |
| List 41 | Words with *th* |
| List 42 | Words starting with *ch-* |
| List 43 | Words with *ch* |
| List 44 | Words ending in *-ch* |
| List 45 | Words ending in *-ce* |
| List 46 | Words with soft *c* or hard *ch* |
| List 47 | Words ending in *-a* or *-o* |
| List 48 | Words with middle *th* |
| Lists 49-50 | More common words |

Kit's Graded Spelling Lists

## YEAR 2    LIST 1

one
two
three
four
five
six
seven
eight
nine
could
would
should
their
talk
walk
want

## YEAR 2    LIST 2

also
after
even
ever
never
very
only
over
often
under
unless
until
hello
know
knew
maybe

### EXTRA WORDS

sixty
seventy
eighty
wouldn't
shouldn't

### EXTRA WORDS

every
everyday
everyone
evenly
overly

## YEAR 2    LIST 3

foe
toe
woe
come
some
done
none
gone
bore
core
more
sore
tore
wore
lose
move

## YEAR 2    LIST 4

bare
care
dare
fare
hare
mare
rare
mere
fire
hire
tire
wire
cure
lure
pure
sure

### EXTRA WORDS

doe
ore
pore
boring
losing

### EXTRA WORDS

dire
mire
wares
purely
surely

## YEAR 2    LIST 5

use
fuse
muse
cube
tube
rude
duke
rule
fume
dune
tune
cute
blue
clue
glue
true

## YEAR 2    LIST 6

who
whom
why
what
when
where
which
whim
whip
whir
whale
wheel
while
white
whisk
whole

## EXTRA WORDS

nude
lute
mute
cue
hue

## EXTRA WORDS

whoa
whiz
whipped
whirred
wheeled

## YEAR 2    LIST 7

they
there
these
those
thank
thing
think
thick
age
cage
page
rage
wage
huge
gel
gem

## YEAR 2    LIST 8

ace
face
lace
pace
race
place
space
grace
ice
dice
mice
nice
rice
slice
spice
price

## EXTRA WORDS

gist
gene
aging
raging
waging

## EXTRA WORDS

lice
brace
trace
racing
slicing

| YEAR 2    LIST 9 | YEAR 2    LIST 10 |
|---|---|
| bass | staff |
| mass | cliff |
| pass | stiff |
| class | stuff |
| glass | small |
| brass | stall |
| grass | smell |
| bless | spell |
| dress | swell |
| press | skill |
| chess | spill |
| bliss | drill |
| floss | frill |
| gloss | grill |
| cross | still |
| across | skull |

| EXTRA WORDS | EXTRA WORDS |
|---|---|
| lass | sniff |
| crass | bluff |
| gross | gruff |
| tresses | dwell |
| glasses | troll |

## YEAR 2    LIST 11

fail
hail
jail
mail
nail
pail
rail
sail
tail
aim
gain
main
pain
rain
bait
wait

## YEAR 2    LIST 12

aid
laid
maid
paid
raid
air
fair
hair
pair
oil
boil
coil
foil
soil
coin
join

### EXTRA WORDS

ail
maim
lain
waiter
sailor

### EXTRA WORDS

lair
toil
void
airy
hairy

## YEAR 2    LIST 13

bye
dye
key
buy
guy
sly
pry
clay
play
fray
gray
pray
tray
stay
sway
prey

## YEAR 2    LIST 14

ear
eat
pea
sea
tea
flea
plea
bead
lead
read
beat
feat
heat
meat
neat
seat

## EXTRA WORDS

rye
sty
bray
slay
ploy

## EXTRA WORDS

pleas
leader
neater
reheat
reread

| YEAR 2    LIST 15 | YEAR 2    LIST 16 |
|---|---|
| oar | hack |
| roar | lack |
| soar | shack |
| load | black |
| road | smack |
| toad | snack |
| loaf | crack |
| soak | track |
| foam | stack |
| roam | chick |
| loan | click |
| moan | flick |
| soap | brick |
| boat | prick |
| coat | trick |
| goat | stick |

| EXTRA WORDS | EXTRA WORDS |
|---|---|
| oaf | slack |
| oak | slick |
| oats | blacken |
| boar | slacken |
| moat | chicken |

## YEAR 2   LIST 17

check
fleck
speck
chock
shock
block
clock
flock
frock
stock
o'clock
chuck
cluck
pluck
truck
stuck

## YEAR 2   LIST 18

flee
glee
free
tree
sleek
creek
green
preen
sleep
creep
steep
sweep
fleet
sleet
greet
sweet

### EXTRA WORDS

smock
unblock
unstuck
checking
shocking

### EXTRA WORDS

twee
tweet
asleep
fleeing
sweeping

## YEAR 2    LIST 19

bleed
speed
breed
creed
freed
greed
steed
tweed
steel
sneer
steer
sleeve
breeze
freeze
sneeze
wheeze

### EXTRA WORDS

greedy
breezy
steering
freezing
sneezing

## YEAR 2    LIST 20

awe
claw
draw
flaw
shawl
crawl
trawl
drawn
prawn
blew
flew
brew
crew
drew
grew
stew

### EXTRA WORDS

slew
brawl
drawl
flawed
brewed

## YEAR 2    LIST 21

brow
prow
fowl
howl
show
blow
flow
glow
slow
snow
crow
grow
stow
bowl
grown
shown

## YEAR 2    LIST 22

crowd
growl
prowl
clown
brown
crown
drown
frown
bloom
gloom
broom
groom
brook
stood
floor
groove

### EXTRA WORDS

blown
flown
flowed
glowed
stowed

### EXTRA WORDS

scowl
crook
crowded
crowned
frowned

## YEAR 2   LIST 23

brood
proof
spool
stool
spoon
scoop
snoop
droop
troop
stoop
swoop
scoot
goose
loose
moose
noose

## YEAR 2   LIST 24

blade
grade
spade
trade
grape
skate
plate
crate
grate
state
bribe
tribe
glide
slide
bride
pride

## EXTRA WORDS

spoof
drool
swoon
drooped
scooped

## EXTRA WORDS

glade
drape
slate
skating
gliding

## YEAR 2    LIST 25

scale
stale
blame
flame
frame
crane
plane
brave
crave
grave
slave
smile
slime
crime
grime
prime

## YEAR 2    LIST 26

spike
trike
gripe
swipe
spite
globe
probe
smoke
spoke
broke
stole
scone
stone
scope
slope
grope

### EXTRA WORDS

stile
slimy
gravy
flaming
craving

### EXTRA WORDS

stoke
clone
drone
prone
snipe

## YEAR 2    LIST 27

flake
snake
brake
stake
spine
brine
swine
twine
drive
close
prose
clove
drove
grove
prove
stove

## YEAR 2    LIST 28

scare
flare
glare
spare
stare
spire
score
snore
store
swore
crude
fluke
plume
prune
brute
flute

### EXTRA WORDS

drake
trove
spinal
closely
proven

### EXTRA WORDS

snare
spore
scary
staring
crudely

## YEAR 2    LIST 29

calf
half
ask
bask
mask
task
calm
palm
gasp
raft
cast
fast
last
mast
past
vast

## YEAR 2    LIST 30

bald
mild
wild
bind
find
kind
mind
rind
wind
folk
yolk
halt
salt
host
most
post

### EXTRA WORDS

cask
rasp
daft
lastly
calmly

### EXTRA WORDS

pint
hind
malt
kindness
baldness

## YEAR 2    LIST 31

fir
sir
stir
bird
girl
firm
dirt
skirt
thirst
cord
lord
born
corn
horn
torn
worn

## YEAR 2    LIST 32

cork
fork
pork
form
norm
fort
port
sort
horse
sword
stork
storm
scorn
thorn
snort
sport

### EXTRA WORDS

irk
swirl
twirl
flirt
stirred

### EXTRA WORDS

horde
sworn
stormy
thorny
sporty

## YEAR 2　　LIST 33

fur
purr
blur
spur
curb
lurk
curl
hurl
burn
turn
curt
hurt
curse
nurse
purse
burst

## YEAR 2　　LIST 34

herb
verb
herd
term
fern
stern
loud
foul
noun
hour
sour
bout
pout
shout
pour
tour

### EXTRA WORDS

urn
slur
blurt
spurt
blurred

### EXTRA WORDS

tern
pert
lout
thou
poured

## YEAR 2   LIST 35

leaf
beak
leak
peak
weak
deal
heal
meal
peal
real
seal
zeal
bean
lean
mean
wean

### EXTRA WORDS

teak
weaker
weakest
weakly
weakling

## YEAR 2   LIST 36

beam
seam
team
heap
leap
reap
dear
fear
gear
hear
near
rear
tear
year
ease
tease

### EXTRA WORDS

sear
easy
easier
easiest
unease

| YEAR 2   LIST 37 | YEAR 2   LIST 38 |
|---|---|
| shade | shark |
| shake | sharp |
| shame | shirt |
| shape | shirk |
| share | shorn |
| shave | short |
| shard | shaft |
| sheen | shelf |
| sheep | shift |
| sheer | shred |
| sheet | shrill |
| shear | shrink |
| shine | shrimp |
| shire | shrine |
| shone | shrub |
| shore | shrug |

| EXTRA WORDS | EXTRA WORDS |
|---|---|
| sheaf | shunt |
| shared | shrewd |
| sheared | shrunk |
| shaking | shredded |
| shining | shrugged |

| YEAR 2 LIST 39 | YEAR 2 LIST 40 |
|---|---|
| bash | blush |
| rash | flush |
| gush | brush |
| hush | crush |
| lush | flesh |
| rush | fresh |
| clash | teeth |
| flash | berth |
| slash | birth |
| smash | booth |
| crash | tooth |
| trash | smooth |
| stash | north |
| harsh | cloth |
| marsh | froth |
| leash | truth |

| EXTRA WORDS | EXTRA WORDS |
|---|---|
| brash | mesh |
| swish | filth |
| plush | girth |
| slush | mirth |
| clashes | broth |

## YEAR 2   LIST 41

thaw
theme
theft
thrash
thrill
thrift
thrive
throb
throng
throne
throw
thrust
bathe
seethe
soothe
clothe

## YEAR 2   LIST 42

chant
chalk
charm
chart
chase
chew
cheek
cheep
cheer
cheese
chest
chide
chime
child
chill
chink

### EXTRA WORDS

thump
thresh
lathe
soothing
clothing

### EXTRA WORDS

chalky
cheery
cheesy
chiding
choking

## YEAR 2  LIST 43

each
beach
peach
reach
teach
chain
chair
cheap
cheat
chirp
choke
chore
chose
choose
chunk
churn

## YEAR 2  LIST 44

arch
march
parch
starch
beech
speech
perch
bleach
preach
birch
brooch
porch
torch
scorch
lurch
church

### EXTRA WORDS

chafe
chump
chosen
choosy
choosing

### EXTRA WORDS

leech
mooch
pooch
torches
lurches

## YEAR 2    LIST 45

once
dance
lance
chance
glance
stance
prance
trance
fence
hence
pence
mince
since
wince
prince
dunce

## YEAR 2    LIST 46

cell
cent
center
city
circle
force
fleece
scene
scent
science
ache
echo
chord
choir
school
scheme

### EXTRA WORDS

twice
thrice
dancing
glancing
wincing

### EXTRA WORDS

farce
scarce
truce
aching
echoing

## YEAR 2    LIST 47

era
soda
sofa
gala
extra
duo
trio
dodo
halo
solo
hero
disco
cargo
banjo
piano
motto

## YEAR 2    LIST 48

gather
lather
father
rather
tether
dither
hither
wither
slither
bother
other
mother
brother
farther
further
another

### EXTRA WORDS

cola
data
veto
mango
bingo

### EXTRA WORDS

slather
panther
fatherly
withered
furthest

## YEAR 2     LIST 49

about
again
alive
along
alone
among
apart
around
away
almost
already
always
nearby
during
within
whether

## YEAR 2     LIST 50

became
become
because
begin
began
begun
before
behind
belong
below
beneath
beside
between
beyond
together
toward

## EXTRA WORDS

lively
lonely
nearly
mostly
partly

## EXTRA WORDS

inside
outside
becoming
beginning
altogether

# YEAR 2    REVISION LIST

| | | |
|---|---|---|
| talk | two | until |
| never | none | eight |
| wire | pure | true |
| want | rude | thick |
| grace | huge | class |
| across | sniff | crow |
| swell | rail | price |
| key | sway | lead |
| thirst | soak | truck |
| creek | bait | neat |
| harsh | chore | tease |
| crawl | sore | stew |
| black | scorch | rear |
| nurse | howl | slope |
| truth | droop | stick |
| loose | skate | frown |
| glance | greed | glide |
| crave | soil | marsh |
| prove | teeth | mean |
| whole | further | brute |
| curl | beyond | hour |
| leak | sword | shrine |
| thrust | flash | snake |
| loud | theft | roar |
| clothe | past | chant |
| fair | cheese | trio |
| sleeve | yolk | wheel |
| kind | waste | sweet |
| prince | city | mother |
| already | stood | during |
| shift | halt | belong |
| palm | toward | again |
| halo | school | rind |
| | science | |

# YEAR 3

## YEAR 3 LIST 1

scar
star
scarf
snarl
spark
stark
smart
start
sparse
carve
starve
terse
verse
nerve
serve
swerve

## YEAR 3 LIST 2

dense
sense
tense
rinse
else
false
pulse
baste
haste
paste
taste
waste
halve
delve
shelve
solve

## EXTRA WORDS

spar
scarring
starring
starving
swerving

## EXTRA WORDS

valve
hasty
tasty
halving
shelving

## YEAR 3    LIST 3

steal
cream
dream
gleam
steam
clean
jeans
clear
smear
spear
peace
cease
lease
crease
grease
please

## YEAR 3    LIST 4

bleak
sneak
speak
creak
freak
tweak
bleat
pleat
treat
east
beast
feast
least
yeast
heath
sheath

### EXTRA WORDS

creasing
greasy
cleared
dreamt
peaceful

### EXTRA WORDS

pleated
speaker
creaky
eastern
beastly

## YEAR 3    LIST 5

dead
head
bread
dread
deaf
sweat
leant
meant
breast
death
breath
breadth
leave
weave
breathe
beard

## YEAR 3    LIST 6

slang
blank
flank
plank
crank
drank
stank
clamp
cramp
tramp
stamp
blink
clink
brink
drink
stink

## EXTRA WORDS

ahead
instead
heave
weaving
breathing

## EXTRA WORDS

prank
slink
blankly
stamped
blinker

## YEAR 3   LIST 7

gland
brand
grand
stand
scalp
brisk
crisp
twist
clung
flung
slung
stung
swung
skunk
drunk
trunk

### EXTRA WORDS

slunk
bland
grander
grandest
grandly

## YEAR 3   LIST 8

bring
cling
fling
sling
sting
swing
crimp
scold
blond
frond
frost
blunt
grunt
stunt
crust
trust

### EXTRA WORDS

skimp
prong
frosty
frostier
frostiest

## YEAR 3   LIST 9

blend
spend
trend
spent
smelt
dwelt
crept
slept
swept
crest
clump
plump
slump
stump
spasm
prism

## YEAR 3   LIST 10

flask
clasp
grasp
craft
grant
plant
slant
blast
blind
drift
swift
spilt
stilt
flint
glint
print

### EXTRA WORDS

trump
frisk
crispy
crispier
crispiest

### EXTRA WORDS

graft
grind
stint
planted
glinted

## YEAR 3     LIST 11

bear
pear
tear
wear
swear
health
wealth
stealth
tread
thread
threat
realm
ready
steady
heavy
heart

### EXTRA WORDS

cleanse
hearth
readily
steadily
heavily

## YEAR 3     LIST 12

earl
early
earn
heard
pearl
learn
yearn
earth
search
break
steak
great
board
broad
coarse
hoarse

### EXTRA WORDS

dearth
hoard
learned
earlier
earliest

| YEAR 3　LIST 13 | YEAR 3　LIST 14 |
|---|---|
| coal | bail |
| foal | wail |
| goal | vain |
| oath | braid |
| cloak | snail |
| croak | frail |
| groan | trail |
| float | claim |
| gloat | plain |
| throat | brain |
| coach | drain |
| poach | grain |
| boast | stain |
| coast | train |
| roast | flair |
| toast | stairs |

| EXTRA WORDS | EXTRA WORDS |
|---|---|
| goad | staid |
| coax | flail |
| hoax | brail |
| coaches | slain |
| poaches | plait |

## YEAR 3    LIST 15

trait
faint
paint
saint
waist
faith
raise
praise
joint
point
hoist
moist
spoil
voice
noise
choice

## YEAR 3    LIST 16

stage
barge
large
charge
badge
cadge
range
change
orange
budge
fudge
judge
nudge
smudge
grudge
trudge

### EXTRA WORDS

gait
taint
oink
poise
foist

### EXTRA WORDS

budge
sludge
barged
ranged
begrudged

## YEAR 3　　LIST 17

urge
purge
surge
bulge
ridge
bridge
fridge
binge
hinge
singe
cringe
fringe
twinge
lunge
plunge
lounge

## YEAR 3　　LIST 18

merge
verge
forge
gorge
edge
hedge
ledge
wedge
pledge
sledge
dredge
dodge
lodge
sponge
scourge
splurge

### EXTRA WORDS

tinge
midge
surging
bridging
plunging

### EXTRA WORDS

dirge
gauge
stodge
merging
edging

| YEAR 3    LIST 19 | YEAR 3    LIST 20 |
|---|---|
| daze | quad |
| faze | quay |
| gaze | qualm |
| haze | quash |
| laze | quake |
| maze | quaint |
| raze | quell |
| size | quest |
| doze | quench |
| blaze | quite |
| glaze | quiet |
| craze | quill |
| froze | quilt |
| prize | quote |
| jazz | quota |
| buzz | quoit |

| EXTRA WORDS | EXTRA WORDS |
|---|---|
| graze | quotas |
| hazy | quenches |
| dozy | quaking |
| lazily | quelling |
| crazily | quoting |

| YEAR 3    LIST 21 | YEAR 3    LIST 22 |
|---|---|
| splash | scrap |
| split | scrape |
| splint | scrawl |
| strap | script |
| straw | screw |
| stray | screen |
| strain | scream |
| strange | scroll |
| street | scrub |
| strip | scrum |
| stride | spray |
| strike | spree |
| stripe | sprig |
| strive | sprain |
| stroll | spread |
| stroke | sprout |

| EXTRA WORDS | EXTRA WORDS |
|---|---|
| splice | sprawl |
| strobe | sprite |
| strapped | spruce |
| stripped | scrapped |
| striped | scraped |

## YEAR 3    LIST 23

strait
stream
streak
stress
stretch
string
strong
struck
strength
length
batch
catch
fetch
itch
ditch
notch

### EXTRA WORDS

strut
strung
lengthen
strengthen
strengthened

## YEAR 3    LIST 24

hatch
latch
match
patch
thatch
snatch
scratch
sketch
hitch
pitch
witch
stitch
switch
hutch
clutch
crutch

### EXTRA WORDS

retch
twitch
blotchy
scratchy
sketchy

## YEAR 3    LIST 25

belch
bench
clench
drench
trench
inch
finch
pinch
winch
flinch
bunch
hunch
lunch
munch
punch
crunch

## YEAR 3    LIST 26

batter
latter
matter
chatter
shatter
scatter
clatter
flatter
platter
splatter
better
letter
bitter
litter
glitter
twitter

### EXTRA WORDS

mulch
stench
clinch
bunches
trenches

### EXTRA WORDS

patter
spatter
fritter
chattered
flattered

## YEAR 3    LIST 27

robber
rubber
blubber
adder
udder
rudder
shudder
utter
butter
gutter
mutter
clutter
flutter
shutter
stutter
splutter

## YEAR 3    LIST 28

offer
differ
suffer
hammer
stammer
inner
banner
manner
dinner
pepper
zipper
flipper
slipper
copper
stopper
supper

## EXTRA WORDS

slobber
fodder
uttered
robbery
rubbery

## EXTRA WORDS

coffer
sinner
winner
snapper
shopper

## YEAR 3    LIST 29

shallow
bellow
fellow
mellow
yellow
billow
pillow
follow
hollow
arrow
barrow
narrow
sparrow
borrow
sorrow
burrow

## YEAR 3    LIST 30

sudden
pollen
sullen
happen
kitten
mitten
coffin
muffin
ribbon
common
summon
cotton
button
blossom
bottom
possum

### EXTRA WORDS

fallow
willow
marrow
barrowful
sorrowful

### EXTRA WORDS

barren
smitten
puffin
gallon
mutton

| YEAR 3     LIST 31 | YEAR 3     LIST 32 |
|---|---|
| channel | pier |
| flannel | tier |
| kennel | view |
| funnel | brief |
| tunnel | chief |
| barrel | grief |
| vessel | thief |
| nugget | field |
| bullet | yield |
| plummet | shield |
| puppet | priest |
| rabbit | niece |
| summit | piece |
| ballot | siege |
| carrot | shriek |
| parrot | friend |

| EXTRA WORDS | EXTRA WORDS |
|---|---|
| fillet | wield |
| maggot | fiend |
| plummeting | chiefs |
| funneling | grieves |
| tunneling | thieves |

## YEAR 3    LIST 33

cloud
proud
shroud
bound
found
hound
mound
pound
round
sound
wound
ground
flour
scour
house
mouse

## YEAR 3    LIST 34

scout
snout
spout
trout
stout
ouch
couch
pouch
vouch
crouch
mouth
south
count
mount
joust
blouse

### EXTRA WORDS

douse
louse
spouse
floury
mousy

### EXTRA WORDS

clout
flout
gout
grouch
slouch

## YEAR 3     LIST 35

soul
soup
group
wound
youth
mourn
court
course
source
ounce
bounce
pounce
young
touch
double
trouble

## YEAR 3     LIST 36

aunt
haul
maul
faun
taut
sauce
cause
pause
clause
fault
vault
haunt
taunt
flaunt
launch
paunch

### EXTRA WORDS

trounce
bouncing
pouncing
soulful
youthful

### EXTRA WORDS

gaunt
saucer
haunches
hauled
mauled

## YEAR 3    LIST 37

area
idea
create
liar
duel
fuel
cruel
poem
alien
diet
duet
fluid
ruin
neon
lion
riot

### EXTRA WORDS

poetry
naive
mosaic
deity
fiord

## YEAR 3    LIST 38

babble
scrabble
nibble
scribble
gobble
hobble
wobble
bubble
rubble
baffle
raffle
ruffle
scuffle
giggle
wiggle
goggle

### EXTRA WORDS

rabble
dribble
cobble
stubble
haggle

## YEAR 3    LIST 39

paddle
saddle
middle
riddle
cuddle
huddle
muddle
puddle
battle
cattle
rattle
kettle
nettle
settle
little
bottle

## YEAR 3    LIST 40

apple
grapple
ripple
cripple
topple
supple
hassle
tussle
dazzle
sizzle
drizzle
grizzle
nozzle
muzzle
nuzzle
puzzle

## EXTRA WORDS

fiddle
griddle
prattle
mettle
throttle

## EXTRA WORDS

fizzle
guzzle
swizzle
dappled
puzzled

## YEAR 3    LIST 41

buggy
rally
tally
jelly
silly
holly
jolly
bully
marry
berry
ferry
merry
cherry
sorry
curry
hurry

## YEAR 3    LIST 42

hobby
lobby
eddy
teddy
giddy
buddy
mommy
dummy
mummy
penny
bunny
funny
happy
choppy
tatty
pretty

### EXTRA WORDS

baggy
shaggy
gully
married
curried

### EXTRA WORDS

cranny
yummy
floppy
sloppy
ditty

## YEAR 3    LIST 43

baby
ruby
lady
body
lily
holy
pity
duty
study
truly
army
party
dainty
plenty
fancy
mercy

## YEAR 3    LIST 44

tiny
pony
puny
vary
wary
bury
fury
jury
posy
rosy
busy
ivy
navy
cozy
glory
story

### EXTRA WORDS

balmy
dingy
lofty
grisly
surly

### EXTRA WORDS

gory
nosy
flimsy
clumsy
curtsy

## YEAR 3   LIST 45

- enter
- banter
- canter
- splinter
- master
- plaster
- fester
- pester
- mister
- sister
- blister
- foster
- roster
- monster
- cluster
- fluster

## YEAR 3   LIST 46

- fiber
- baker
- shaker
- poker
- cater
- later
- meter
- liter
- crater
- garter
- porter
- oyster
- layer
- player
- prayer
- foyer

### EXTRA WORDS

- caster
- muster
- bluster
- lobster
- specter

### EXTRA WORDS

- bunker
- busker
- rooster
- neuter
- pewter

## YEAR 3     LIST 47

order
border
girder
murder
spider
slander
slender
tinder
ponder
blunder
plunder
thunder
boarder
former
corner
partner

## YEAR 3     LIST 48

badger
danger
ginger
finger
linger
tiger
hunger
fever
sever
clever
river
liver
shiver
silver
hover
clover

## EXTRA WORDS

larder
blender
farmer
formerly
orderly

## EXTRA WORDS

wager
burger
lever
rover
sliver

## YEAR 3    LIST 49

paper
viper
barber
clamber
chamber
member
timber
somber
number
slumber
hamper
tamper
scamper
temper
proper
prosper

## YEAR 3    LIST 50

himself
herself
anyone
anyway
anywhere
no-one
nowhere
someone
somewhere
forever
whoever
whenever
wherever
otherwise
meanwhile
therefore

### EXTRA WORDS

wiper
amber
pamper
slumbered
prospered

### EXTRA WORDS

yourselves
themselves
nobody
anybody
somebody

# YEAR 3    REVISION LIST

| | | |
|---|---|---|
| spark | verse | swung |
| least | spasm | crouch |
| clear | trust | pretty |
| coarse | swift | slept |
| craft | dread | siege |
| spread | burrow | surge |
| choice | grease | fluid |
| prize | froze | breath |
| cuddle | stamp | quake |
| stroke | health | scrawl |
| twist | stairs | large |
| struck | wound | speak |
| piano | match | busy |
| clench | later | strange |
| stammer | quench | slumber |
| plank | drizzle | sorrow |
| mercy | house | sponge |
| common | priest | slipper |
| fudge | joust | friend |
| puzzle | lunch | sudden |
| marry | pounce | giggle |
| bridge | mutter | quiet |
| kennel | wobble | view |
| scratch | scribble | ledge |
| topple | nobody | cruel |
| sorry | notch | hunger |
| holy | halve | parrot |
| monster | penny | murder |
| duty | plunder | cause |
| cluster | source | prayer |
| vessel | prosper | thunder |
| nowhere | shiver | otherwise |
| neuter | yellow | cherry |
| | paste | |

# YEAR 4

| List 1 | Words for numbers |
|---|---|
| Lists 2-5 | Words ending in -*le* |
| List 6 | Words with *ck* |
| List 7 | Words ending in -*et* |
| Lists 8-13 | Words ending in a single consonant |
| List 14 | Words ending in -*ic* |
| List 15 | Words ending in -*id* |
| Lists 16-17 | Words ending in -*al* |
| List 18 | Words ending in -*el* or -*il* |
| List 19 | Words ending in -*el* or -*ol* |
| List 20 | Words ending in -*ial* |
| List 21 | Words ending in -*y* |
| List 22 | Words ending in -*ay* or -*oy* |
| List 23 | Words with *x* and *z* |
| Lists 24-25 | Words with *qu* |
| List 26 | Words starting with *wh-* |
| List 27 | Words with *ph* |
| Lists 28-29 | Words with silent letters |
| List 30 | Words with *igh* |
| List 31 | Words with *ough* |
| List 32 | Words starting with *wr-* |
| Lists 33-35 | Words with unusual vowel sounds |
| List 36 | Words with *ow* |
| List 37 | Words ending in -*ow*, -*ew* and -*aw* |
| List 38 | Words with *ai* |
| List 39 | Words with *ea* |
| List 40 | Words with *ie* |
| List 41 | Words with *ei* |
| List 42 | Words with *ui* |
| List 43 | Words with common prefixes: *a-* and *ad-* |
| List 44 | Words with common prefixes: *com-* and *con-* |
| List 45 | Words with common prefixes: *de-* and *dis-* |
| List 46 | Words with common prefixes: *ex-*, *im-* and *in-* |
| List 47 | Words with common prefixes: *per-*, *pre-* and *pro-* |
| List 48 | Words with common prefixes: *re-* |
| List 49 | Words for days and numbers |
| List 50 | Words for times of the day or year |

## YEAR 4    LIST 1

eleven
twelve
thirteen
fourteen
fifteen
sixteen
seventeen
eighteen
nineteen
twenty
thirty
forty
fifty
hundred
thousand
million
billion
trillion

## YEAR 4    LIST 2

able
cable
fable
table
stable
bible
noble
marble
feeble
gamble
scramble
tremble
nimble
thimble
humble
mumble
crumble
stumble

## EXTRA WORDS

twenty-one
thirty-two
forty-three
millionth
billionth

## EXTRA WORDS

ramble
treble
fumble
rumble
grumble

## YEAR 4    LIST 3

ladle
cradle
needle
candle
handle
kindle
fondle
bundle
ample
sample
temple
dimple
simple
staple
steeple
people
triple
purple

## YEAR 4    LIST 4

angle
bangle
dangle
tangle
strangle
jingle
mingle
single
burgle
gurgle
title
beetle
startle
turtle
castle
nestle
bustle
rustle

## EXTRA WORDS

maple
spindle
dwindle
cradling
sampling

## EXTRA WORDS

mangle
tingle
mantle
jostle
hurtle

## YEAR 4    LIST 5

trifle
stifle
ankle
sparkle
twinkle
sprinkle
cackle
tackle
crackle
shackle
freckle
fickle
pickle
tickle
prickle
trickle
buckle
chuckle

## YEAR 4    LIST 6

beckon
reckon
bicker
wicker
sticker
jacket
packet
racket
bracket
ticket
wicket
thicket
cricket
locket
pocket
rocket
socket
bucket

## EXTRA WORDS

rifle
crinkle
heckle
suckle
speckled

## EXTRA WORDS

cracker
docket
picket
bracketed
pocketed

## YEAR 4   LIST 7

cadet
target
forget
basket
blanket
tablet
triplet
violet
toilet
racquet
helmet
magnet
planet
carpet
trumpet
secret
closet
velvet

## YEAR 4   LIST 8

urban
turban
organ
human
habit
orbit
edit
credit
digit
limit
hermit
permit
unit
merit
spirit
culprit
robot
pivot

### EXTRA WORDS

casket
trinket
hatchet
goblet
bracelet

### EXTRA WORDS

bigot
pagan
emit
spirited
merited

## YEAR 4    LIST 9

burden
garden
linen
open
siren
children
haven
raven
heaven
kitchen
cabin
robin
napkin
pumpkin
violin
basin
raisin
satin

### EXTRA WORDS

token
goblin
omen
vermin
vitamin

## YEAR 4    LIST 10

icon
bacon
pardon
wagon
dragon
salon
melon
nylon
demon
lemon
cannon
iron
apron
crimson
person
baton
crayon
canyon

### EXTRA WORDS

flagon
colon
coupon
heron
prison

## YEAR 4    LIST 11

item
denim
victim
atom
venom
seldom
random
wisdom
freedom
ransom
custom
forum
album
emblem
problem
pilgrim
spectrum
tantrum

## YEAR 4    LIST 12

superb
proverb
shepherd
modern
lantern
pattern
cavern
govern
tavern
inert
overt
concert
expert
assert
insert
covert
convert
subvert

### EXTRA WORDS

totem
maxim
fathom
tandem
mayhem

### EXTRA WORDS

berserk
discern
cistern
lectern
revert

## YEAR 4    LIST 13

ragged
dogged
rugged
wicked
crooked
sacred
hatred
kindred
method
period
serif
motif
tulip
turnip
parsnip
gossip
gallop
bishop

## YEAR 4    LIST 14

mimic
comic
panic
sonic
tonic
topic
music
basic
critic
attic
toxic
ethic
traffic
italic
frolic
garlic
public
hectic

### EXTRA WORDS

naked
scallop
dollop
methodical
periodical

### EXTRA WORDS

cubic
relic
antic
mimicking
panicking

## YEAR 4    LIST 15

acid
placid
lucid
rigid
frigid
valid
solid
timid
humid
rapid
stupid
horrid
putrid
livid
vivid
morbid
sordid
splendid

## YEAR 4    LIST 16

focal
local
vocal
medal
pedal
legal
regal
frugal
canal
final
oral
coral
moral
floral
spiral
mural
rural
plural

## EXTRA WORDS

rabid
acrid
torrid
rigidity
stupidity

## EXTRA WORDS

verbal
bridal
feudal
feral
rascal

## YEAR 4    LIST 17

sandal
scandal
formal
normal
fatal
petal
metal
vital
total
mental
mortal
oval
rival
loyal
royal
animal
several
hospital

## YEAR 4    LIST 18

model
cancel
parcel
lapel
chapel
repel
easel
weasel
tinsel
tassel
hotel
pastel
pencil
pupil
peril
fossil
devil
nostril

## EXTRA WORDS

dismal
brutal
festival
formality
totality

## EXTRA WORDS

morsel
vigil
basil
tonsil
tendril

## YEAR 4    LIST 19

label
rebel
camel
panel
kernel
level
revel
swivel
hovel
novel
gravel
travel
marvel
jewel
idol
carol
patrol
control

## YEAR 4    LIST 20

dial
trial
special
social
crucial
official
cordial
genial
menial
serial
burial
partial
spatial
jovial
trivial
material
initial
essential

### EXTRA WORDS

libel
chisel
navel
grovel
gospel

### EXTRA WORDS

memorial
tutorial
potential
triviality
joviality

## YEAR 4    LIST 21

- ugly
- envy
- treaty
- empty
- beauty
- family
- enemy
- colony
- misery
- sanity
- vanity
- purity
- cavity
- gravity
- liberty
- property
- poverty
- galaxy

## YEAR 4    LIST 22

- allay
- array
- essay
- hooray
- delay
- mislay
- dismay
- display
- astray
- betray
- portray
- decoy
- enjoy
- annoy
- convoy
- deploy
- employ
- destroy

## EXTRA WORDS

- legacy
- fallacy
- canopy
- embassy
- jewelry

## EXTRA WORDS

- foray
- heyday
- outlay
- betrayal
- portrayal

## YEAR 4    LIST 23

vex
relax
index
flux
zone
zero
zebra
zigzag
hazel
dizzy
frenzy
bronze
frieze
snooze
blazer
trapeze
bazaar
bizarre

## YEAR 4    LIST 24

quail
queue
quarry
quarrel
quarter
query
queasy
question
quibble
quirk
quiver
qualify
quality
quantity
equal
tranquil
enquire
require

### EXTRA WORDS

apex
annex
fizzy
gauze
tweezers

### EXTRA WORDS

quartz
queued
qualified
quarreled
quivered

## YEAR 4    LIST 25

squad
squat
square
squash
squeeze
squeak
squeal
squid
squint
squire
squirm
squirt
squabble
squalor
squander
squirrel
liquid
conquer

## YEAR 4    LIST 26

whack
wharf
whet
wheat
whence
whiff
whilst
whine
whirl
wheedle
whimper
whimsy
whinny
whisker
whisper
whistle
whittle
whereas

## EXTRA WORDS

squall
squelch
squatting
squeezing
squirreling

## EXTRA WORDS

whoop
whopper
whirling
whining
whistling

## YEAR 4    LIST 27

phase
phrase
phone
phantom
pharaoh
phoenix
physics
physical
sphere
sphinx
orphan
dolphin
elephant
emphasis
triumph
trophy
graph
photograph

### EXTRA WORDS

phobia
pheasant
periphery
autograph
telegraph

## YEAR 4    LIST 28

soften
fasten
hasten
listen
glisten
moisten
island
knack
knee
kneel
knelt
knead
knit
knife
knob
knot
knock
knuckle

### EXTRA WORDS

knell
knoll
knave
softened
fastened

## YEAR 4   LIST 29

sign
lamb
limb
climb
bomb
comb
tomb
dumb
numb
crumb
thumb
debt
doubt
subtle
yacht
stalk
column
answer

## YEAR 4   LIST 30

high
sigh
thigh
bight
fight
light
might
night
right
sight
tight
bright
flight
fright
plight
slight
height
knight

### EXTRA WORDS

design
resign
psalm
almond
salmon

### EXTRA WORDS

blight
lightning
brightening
frightening
tightening

## YEAR 4    LIST 31

ought
bought
fought
sought
thought
brought
dough
though
although
bough
drought
cough
rough
tough
trough
enough
through
thorough

## YEAR 4    LIST 32

wrap
wrath
wreath
wren
wreck
wrench
wretch
write
wrote
written
wring
wrist
wrong
wrung
wrangle
wrestle
wriggle
wrinkle

## EXTRA WORDS

thoughtless
thoughtlessness
thoughtful
thoughtfully
thoughtfulness

## EXTRA WORDS

wry
wrathful
wrongful
wriggling
wrinkling

## YEAR 4    LIST 33

- dove
- glove
- shove
- above
- lovely
- honey
- dozen
- money
- monk
- monkey
- month
- oven
- cover
- blood
- flood
- front
- comfort
- company

## YEAR 4    LIST 34

- wad
- wan
- waft
- wand
- wash
- wasp
- war
- ward
- warn
- wart
- water
- watch
- waltz
- wander
- wardrobe
- warrior
- dwarf
- thwart

## EXTRA WORDS

- shovel
- smother
- lovelier
- loveliest
- loveliness

## EXTRA WORDS

- wanly
- warden
- watery
- watchful
- dwarfed

## YEAR 4     LIST 35

swab
swan
swap
swat
swarm
swamp
word
work
worm
world
worse
worst
worship
worthy
wonder
worry
woman
women

### EXTRA WORDS

worthier
worthiest
worsen
worsened
worsening

## YEAR 4     LIST 36

meow
bower
cower
power
tower
flower
shower
powder
dowdy
rowdy
downy
dowry
drowsy
bowel
vowel
towel
trowel
prowess

### EXTRA WORDS

rowdier
dowdiest
flowery
drowsily
empowered

## YEAR 4   LIST 37

guffaw
jigsaw
mildew
curfew
askew
nephew
cashew
allow
endow
elbow
widow
shadow
meadow
window
bungalow
bestow
wallow
swallow

## YEAR 4   LIST 38

daily
dairy
fairy
daisy
afraid
mermaid
detail
obtain
curtain
fountain
maintain
mountain
entertain
campaign
affair
despair
repair
portrait

### EXTRA WORDS

shadowy
swallowed
bestowal
allowance
endowment

### EXTRA WORDS

prairie
villain
sustain
mountainous
villainous

## YEAR 4    LIST 39

eager
meager
beaker
sneaker
streamer
beaver
beacon
reason
season
treason
weary
dreary
sweater
feather
heather
leather
weather
weapon

## YEAR 4    LIST 40

fierce
pierce
belief
relief
mischief
glacier
soldier
courier
cashier
frontier
sieve
grieve
achieve
believe
relieve
reprieve
retrieve
handkerchief

## EXTRA WORDS

bleary
cleaver
measles
wearily
drearily

## EXTRA WORDS

piercing
sieving
believing
grievous
mischievous

## YEAR 4    LIST 41

heir
rein
vein
reign
feign
foreign
sovereign
conceive
deceive
perceive
receive
conceit
either
neither
seize
seizure
sheik
weird

## YEAR 4    LIST 42

build
guild
built
guilt
guide
guile
guise
disguise
juice
fruit
suit
bruise
cruise
biscuit
circuit
pursuit
recruit
suite

### EXTRA WORDS

weir
skein
heist
feisty
protein

### EXTRA WORDS

juicy
fruity
guilty
guiding
beguiling

## YEAR 4    LIST 43

abroad
alarm
alert
amend
amount
amuse
await
award
aware
adapt
adopt
adore
adhere
admit
adjust
advance
advice
advise

### EXTRA WORDS

abide
align
amass
adept
adverse

## YEAR 4    LIST 44

combine
compare
compel
compute
conceal
concept
concern
conclude
conduct
confess
confide
confine
confirm
conform
confuse
consist
contain
convict

### EXTRA WORDS

conspire
comprise
contort
converse
computer

## YEAR 4    LIST 45

decide
declare
deduce
deduct
defeat
defer
define
deliver
depart
depose
describe
devote
discover
discuss
disease
disgust
dismiss
dispute

### EXTRA WORDS

derive
detain
discord
discount
disrupt

## YEAR 4    LIST 46

exceed
excel
except
excite
exclaim
excuse
exile
express
extend
import
impose
impress
include
inflame
inform
insist
instruct
inverse

### EXTRA WORDS

exchange
impart
incite
infuse
insure

## YEAR 4    LIST 47

persist
pervade
precise
preclude
predict
prefer
prelude
prepare
present
presence
prevail
preview
proclaim
product
profess
promote
provide
provoke

### EXTRA WORDS

prediction
production
profession
promotion
presentation

## YEAR 4    LIST 48

recite
record
recoil
reduce
refine
refuse
regret
remind
remote
repeat
repent
reply
report
resist
respond
restrain
result
reveal

### EXTRA WORDS

relay
repeal
retain
return
review

## YEAR 4     LIST 49

Monday
Tuesday
Wednesday
Thursday
Friday
Saturday
Sunday
today
tomorrow
yesterday
first
second
third
fourth
fifth
eighth
primary
secondary

## YEAR 4     LIST 50

January
February
March
April
May
June
July
August
September
October
November
December
spring
summer
autumn
winter
morning
evening

### EXTRA WORDS

eleventh
twelfth
twentieth
thirtieth
fortieth

### EXTRA WORDS

afternoon
fortnight
midday
holiday
birthday

# YEAR 4    REVISION LIST

| | | |
|---|---|---|
| grumble | jingle | jewel |
| zebra | fifty | moral |
| bucket | billion | digit |
| heaven | canyon | sphere |
| freckle | kitchen | pumpkin |
| leather | presence | dozen |
| whirl | custom | lantern |
| frolic | material | question |
| thimble | vivid | final |
| circuit | several | money |
| despair | rustle | purity |
| wriggle | violet | galaxy |
| receive | fossil | initial |
| portray | pilgrim | conceal |
| swivel | quarrel | cricket |
| inverse | orphan | hospital |
| physics | thought | listen |
| twinkle | squeal | knife |
| neither | August | stalk |
| basket | sight | destroy |
| worst | enough | written |
| front | wrath | worry |
| gossip | whisper | December |
| dreary | amount | crazy |
| thumb | bundle | express |
| curtain | respond | height |
| disturb | parcel | foreign |
| remind | trivial | query |
| guide | flower | knock |
| advance | compel | describe |
| nephew | precise | wrong |
| tomorrow | liquid | season |
| third | Saturday | excite |
| | company | |

# YEAR 5

# YEAR 5, cont/...

## YEAR 5    LIST 1

drama
dogma
comma
china
lava
replica
agenda
veranda
koala
formula
gorilla
umbrella
aroma
diploma
banana
sultana
arena
tiara

## YEAR 5    LIST 2

radar
cedar
sugar
polar
solar
sonar
lunar
altar
beggar
cellar
pillar
collar
dollar
grammar
vulgar
burglar
nectar
guitar

## EXTRA WORDS

panda
puma
llama
tuna
tarantula

## EXTRA WORDS

hangar
caviar
poplar
sugary
burglary

## YEAR 5   LIST 3

tornado
indigo
flamingo
buffalo
volcano
inferno
potato
tomato
lasso
cameo
rodeo
stereo
radio
studio
patio
ratio
cocoa
canoe

## YEAR5   LIST 4

iris
axis
basis
crisis
oasis
thesis
tennis
focus
locus
minus
bonus
rumpus
virus
walrus
citrus
census
status
cactus

## EXTRA WORDS

oboe
radios
volcanos
potatoes
tomatoes

## EXTRA WORDS

abacus
axes
crises
cactuses
viruses

## YEAR 5   LIST 5

coffee
toffee
refugee
jubilee
marquee
referee
guarantee
employee
chimpanzee
decree
agree
degree
pedigree
genie
eerie
calorie
reverie
pixie

## YEAR 5   LIST 6

taboo
bamboo
cuckoo
igloo
shampoo
kangaroo
tattoo
baboon
cocoon
tycoon
lagoon
balloon
harpoon
typhoon
maroon
monsoon
platoon
cartoon

## EXTRA WORDS

yippee
nominee
escapee
refereed
guaranteed

## EXTRA WORDS

voodoo
kazoo
buffoon
raccoon
festoon

## YEAR 5    LIST 7

rescue
argue
value
venue
avenue
continue
pursue
issue
tissue
statue
virtue
perfume
volume
presume
assume
costume
immune
fortune

### EXTRA WORDS

barbecue
residue
revenue
consume
resume

## YEAR 5    LIST 8

taxi
chilli
bikini
safari
privacy
prophecy
policy
vacancy
emergency
currency
allergy
energy
strategy
economy
harmony
fantasy
courtesy
industry

### EXTRA WORDS

broccoli
pharmacy
penalty
warranty
tapestry

## YEAR 5    LIST 9

malady
tragedy
remedy
comedy
melody
parody
custody
jeopardy
mutiny
scrutiny
destiny
agony
balcony
dignity
charity
vitality
frivolity
calamity

## YEAR 5    LIST 10

abbey
alley
galley
valley
volley
trolley
pulley
barley
jersey
hockey
jockey
donkey
turkey
medley
parsley
kidney
chimney
paisley

### EXTRA WORDS

humility
futility
jeopardize
scrutinize
agonize

### EXTRA WORDS

motley
chutney
attorney
valleys
chimneys

## YEAR 5     LIST 11

defy
rely
ally
deny
lullaby
modify
amplify
simplify
magnify
petrify
terrify
horrify
justify
satisfy
occupy
apply
supply
multiply

## YEAR 5     LIST 12

picnic
classic
tactic
frantic
plastic
rustic
organic
fanatic
dramatic
automatic
republic
gigantic
elastic
fantastic
domestic
fabric
metric
electric

### EXTRA WORDS

stupefy
specify
glorify
horrific
terrific

### EXTRA WORDS

civic
aerobic
heretic
fanatical
electrical

## YEAR 5    LIST 13

defect
infect
perfect
prefect
affect
effect
aspect
expect
inspect
prospect
respect
suspect
erect
direct
correct
deflect
inflect
reflect

## YEAR 5    LIST 14

eject
inject
object
project
reject
subject
interject
elect
select
neglect
dialect
collect
intellect
insect
dissect
intersect
detect
protect

## EXTRA WORDS

effective
reflective
perfection
direction
correction

## EXTRA WORDS

objective
selective
rejection
intersection
protection

## YEAR 5    LIST 15

enact
exact
react
transact
interact
counteract
compact
impact
contact
intact
abstract
attract
contract
detract
distract
extract
retract
subtract

## YEAR 5    LIST 16

modest
infest
manifest
digest
ingest
suggest
molest
honest
earnest
forest
interest
arrest
attest
contest
detest
protest
harvest
invest

### EXTRA WORDS

interactive
attractive
abstraction
distraction
subtraction

### EXTRA WORDS

modesty
honesty
digestion
suggestion
manifestation

## YEAR 5   LIST 17

- client
- trident
- strident
- prudent
- student
- accident
- resident
- president
- evident
- content
- extent
- intent
- patent
- potent
- portent
- event
- invent
- prevent

## YEAR 5   LIST 18

- decent
- recent
- ascent
- descent
- pungent
- urgent
- silent
- excellent
- permanent
- continent
- serpent
- eloquent
- parent
- torrent
- current
- consent
- resent
- represent

### EXTRA WORDS

- intention
- prevention
- residential
- presidential
- potentially

### EXTRA WORDS

- ardent
- assent
- relent
- eminent
- insistent

## YEAR 5    LIST 19

abundant
infant
stagnant
remnant
resonant
consonant
flippant
currant
peasant
pleasant
distant
instant
important
servant
relevant
merchant
flagrant
fragrant

## YEAR 5    LIST 20

debate
vacate
locate
sedate
relate
collate
irate
pirate
indicate
delicate
complicate
duplicate
allocate
educate
chocolate
desolate
isolate
calculate

## EXTRA WORDS

warrant
incessant
importance
relevance
fragrance

## EXTRA WORDS

vacation
location
complication
isolation
calculation

## YEAR 5    LIST 21

rotate
dictate
separate
tolerate
operate
desperate
decorate
imitate
irritate
hesitate
vibrate
celebrate
migrate
frustrate
illustrate
graduate
evaluate
situate

## YEAR 5    LIST 22

climate
primate
inmate
innate
ornate
animate
ultimate
estimate
fascinate
nominate
fortunate
designate
delete
athlete
compete
complete
concrete
discrete

## EXTRA WORDS

estate
demonstrate
separation
desperation
graduation

## EXTRA WORDS

stalemate
secrete
estimation
competition
discretion

## YEAR 5    LIST 23

polite
finite
ignite
invite
satellite
dynamite
infinite
favorite
opposite
appetite
acute
salute
pollute
minute
astute
execute
resolute
absolute

### EXTRA WORDS

ignition
invitation
politely
infinitely
absolutely

## YEAR 5    LIST 24

figure
measure
pleasure
treasure
leisure
pressure
mature
nature
future
creature
feature
fracture
lecture
picture
capture
pasture
gesture
texture

### EXTRA WORDS

endure
censure
displeasure
immature
unnatural

## YEAR 5    LIST 25

welfare
warfare
admire
empire
umpire
vampire
desire
satire
retire
entire
aspire
inspire
perspire
galore
ignore
explore
implore
restore

## YEAR 5    LIST 26

major
tremor
manor
minor
stupor
terror
mirror
horror
censor
mayor
author
corridor
alligator
elevator
escalator
junior
senior
superior

## EXTRA WORDS

attire
sapphire
carnivore
inspiration
exploration

## EXTRA WORDS

inferior
exterior
interior
majority
minority

## YEAR 5    LIST 27

tenor
tutor
doctor
traitor
razor
governor
emperor
sponsor
creator
operator
narrator
dictator
spectator
translator
calculator
illustrator
editor
ancestor

### EXTRA WORDS

captor
mentor
monitor
professor
competitor

## YEAR 5    LIST 28

harbor
odor
rigor
vigor
valor
color
parlor
clamor
glamor
humor
rumor
armor
honor
favor
flavor
splendor
savior
behavior

### EXTRA WORDS

vapor
savor
endeavor
glamorous
humorous

## YEAR 5    LIST 29

station
lotion
motion
notion
potion
emotion
portion
caution
action
auction
fraction
section
diction
fiction
friction
function
junction
mention

### EXTRA WORDS

ration
suction
caption
rational
functional

## YEAR 5    LIST 30

inhale
exhale
female
morale
mobile
facile
defile
profile
agile
fragile
senile
compile
missile
reptile
fertile
hostile
crocodile
versatile

### EXTRA WORDS

imbecile
turnstile
agility
facility
hostility

## YEAR 5     LIST 31

cajole
console
globule
module
nodule
granule
capsule
molecule
ridicule
minuscule
adult
exult
occult
tumult
consult
insult
difficult
catapult

## YEAR 5     LIST 32

promise
chastise
surprise
exercise
paradise
realize
baptize
criticize
mobilize
utilize
idolize
organize
recognize
summarize
memorize
authorize
apologize
rationalize

### EXTRA WORDS

rissole
rigmarole
casserole
exultant
consultant

### EXTRA WORDS

compromise
hypnotize
realization
utilization
organization

## YEAR 5    LIST 33

rubbish
brandish
blemish
skirmish
banish
vanish
finish
punish
tarnish
furnish
perish
flourish
nourish
lavish
abolish
demolish
publish
replenish

## YEAR 5    LIST 34

harass
morass
compass
trespass
canvass
process
caress
duress
witness
regress
digress
progress
depress
distress
mattress
encompass
embarrass
wilderness

## EXTRA WORDS

prudish
sluggish
sheepish
gibberish
famished

## EXTRA WORDS

congress
repress
procession
progression
depression

## YEAR 5    LIST 35

ceiling
celery
century
cereal
certain
certify
ceremony
cider
cinder
cinema
circus
citizen
ocean
cancer
grocer
decimal
ancient
innocent

### EXTRA WORDS

civil
facet
ulcer
centenary
citadel

## YEAR 5    LIST 36

chaos
chasm
character
chemist
chorus
chrome
chronicle
schedule
scholar
anchor
archive
orchid
orchestra
loch
epoch
stomach
anarchy
monarchy

### EXTRA WORDS

chronic
schism
ochre
anarchic
monarchic

## YEAR 5    LIST 37

- cherub
- chivalry
- chute
- bachelor
- brochure
- machine
- ostrich
- sandwich
- avalanche
- mustache
- muscle
- scepter
- scenery
- scissors
- coalesce
- crescent
- disciple
- discipline

## YEAR 5    LIST 38

- gym
- gypsy
- hymn
- myth
- style
- type
- thyme
- bicycle
- cylinder
- dynasty
- hybrid
- hydrant
- hygiene
- hyphen
- mystery
- mystify
- typical
- tyrant

## EXTRA WORDS

- scenic
- machinery
- chivalrous
- muscular
- disciplinary

## EXTRA WORDS

- nymph
- scythe
- hyena
- pygmy
- oxygen

## YEAR 5　　LIST 39

crypt
crystal
cycle
cymbal
lyrics
pyramid
python
rhyme
rhythm
syllable
symbol
symmetry
sympathy
symphony
symptom
syringe
syrup
system

## YEAR 5　　LIST 40

loiter
poison
porpoise
turmoil
turquoise
bounty
county
council
boundary
journey
journal
sojourn
country
couple
courage
cousin
tourist
poultry

### EXTRA WORDS

martyr
satyr
odyssey
rhythmic
sympathetic

### EXTRA WORDS

tortoise
detour
contour
courageous
poisonous

## YEAR 5    LIST 41

- aural
- trauma
- sauna
- nausea
- saunter
- sausage
- cauldron
- exhaust
- laundry
- daunting
- nautical
- audible
- plausible
- dinosaur
- centaur
- astronaut
- assault
- somersault

## YEAR 5    LIST 42

- neigh
- weigh
- sleigh
- weight
- freight
- straight
- neighbor
- caught
- naught
- taught
- fraught
- haughty
- naughty
- daughter
- slaughter
- laugh
- laughter
- borough

### EXTRA WORDS

- audition
- gauntlet
- default
- automobile
- autobiography

### EXTRA WORDS

- weighing
- laughing
- naughtier
- naughtiest
- naughtiness

## YEAR 5    LIST 43

gnat
gnaw
gnash
gnarled
gnome
aghast
ghastly
ghost
ghoul
guard
guess
guest
anguish
languish
language
penguin
distinguish
extinguish

### EXTRA WORDS

gnu
languid
linguist
ghastliness
ghostliness

## YEAR 5    LIST 44

magic
tragic
logic
margin
origin
angel
algebra
budget
gadget
pigeon
dungeon
surgeon
pageant
gentle
gender
general
giant
giraffe

### EXTRA WORDS

fidget
midget
bludgeon
genetic
geometry

## YEAR 5   LIST 45

image
damage
manage
garage
forage
storage
savage
message
passage
village
cottage
bandage
rampage
average
hostage
heritage
carriage
marriage

## YEAR 5   LIST 46

vague
plague
rogue
league
colleague
fatigue
intrigue
dialogue
prologue
monologue
catalogue
synagogue
harangue
tongue
analogy
apology
biology
ecology

## EXTRA WORDS

pillage
vintage
beverage
outrage
messenger

## EXTRA WORDS

geology
astrology
zoology
plaguing
haranguing

## YEAR 5   LIST 47

plaque
clique
mosque
brusque
opaque
unique
oblique
physique
antique
critique
boutique
mystique
technique
grotesque
picturesque
conquest
inquest
request

## YEAR 5   LIST 48

acquit
acquaint
acquire
equip
equate
adequate
equator
inquiry
frequent
exquisite
masquerade
quagmire
quarantine
sequin
sequel
sequence
consequence
subsequent

### EXTRA WORDS

critical
technical
mystical
uniquely
obliquely

### EXTRA WORDS

piquant
quadrangle
quotation
adequacy
frequency

## YEAR 5    LIST 49

accent
accept
access
announce
appeal
appear
applause
appoint
approach
approve
attack
attach
attend
attempt
command
commit
commence
comment

## YEAR 5    LIST 50

account
accuse
address
afford
arrange
arrive
assemble
assess
assist
connect
dissolve
effort
oppose
possess
success
suppose
support
surround

### EXTRA WORDS

allege
allure
appalled
appliance
attain

### EXTRA WORDS

acclaim
accrue
affirm
asset
assure

# YEAR 5     REVISION LIST

| | | |
|---|---|---|
| collar | indigo | budget |
| crisis | sultana | referee |
| shampoo | harmony | nectar |
| privacy | chimney | statue |
| citrus | employee | satisfy |
| automatic | expect | neglect |
| distract | interact | interest |
| resident | valley | domestic |
| excellent | current | important |
| system | chocolate | delete |
| illustrate | fracture | ignore |
| suggest | grocer | junior |
| translator | accident | honor |
| fragile | magnify | pollute |
| fragrant | council | formula |
| mention | module | equator |
| compete | gnome | intrigue |
| electric | infinite | cocoa |
| approach | tongue | mirror |
| scenery | organize | nourish |
| success | surprise | apology |
| dissect | demolish | distress |
| certify | unique | dissolve |
| orchid | marriage | machine |
| naughty | tumult | calculate |
| bicycle | message | hyphen |
| rhythm | astronaut | journal |
| plausible | editor | compass |
| straight | stomach | splendor |
| caught | language | general |
| mystery | witness | frequent |
| approve | address | antique |
| gentle | daunting | poison |
| | character | |

# YEAR 6

# YEAR 6, cont/...

## YEAR 6    LIST 1

calendar
vinegar
similar
circular
angular
regular
singular
popular
particular
spectacular
stellar
caterpillar
seminar
linear
nuclear
familiar
peculiar
jaguar

## YEAR 6    LIST 2

bombard
regard
haggard
tankard
leopard
leotard
custard
mustard
reward
coward
backward
forward
awkward
wayward
hazard
lizard
wizard
blizzard

## EXTRA WORDS

jocular
secular
perpendicular
circularity
popularity

## EXTRA WORDS

haphazard
bombardment
regardless
cowardly
awkwardness

## YEAR 6    LIST 3

deface
efface
preface
surface
interface
palace
solace
populace
grimace
menace
furnace
terrace
embrace
disgrace
displace
replace
cyberspace
hyperspace

### EXTRA WORDS

typeface
necklace
resurfaced
disgraceful
displacement

## YEAR 6    LIST 4

device
entice
suffice
sacrifice
crevice
malice
notice
novice
office
practice
police
service
cowardice
prejudice
artifice
precipice
apprentice
accomplice

### EXTRA WORDS

bodice
edifice
solstice
artificial
sacrificial

## YEAR 6     LIST 5

cursive
massive
passive
native
motive
furtive
captive
festive
adhesive
decisive
elusive
creative
talkative
relative
negative
alternative
positive
fugitive

## YEAR 6     LIST 6

turbine
feline
canine
divine
porcupine
valentine
vaccine
sardine
marine
routine
ravine
trampoline
tangerine
margarine
nectarine
tambourine
limousine
magazine

## EXTRA WORDS

cohesive
effusive
passivity
festivity
negativity

## EXTRA WORDS

ermine
doctrine
divinely
divinity
divination

## YEAR 6    LIST 7

engine
jasmine
medicine
imagine
masculine
determine
feminine
genuine
trombone
condone
cyclone
hormone
postpone
monotone
homophone
microphone
telephone
xylophone

### EXTRA WORDS

femininity
masculinity
medication
determination
imagination

## YEAR 6    LIST 8

arcade
decade
cascade
brigade
grenade
charade
parade
crusade
evade
invade
barricade
cavalcade
marmalade
serenade
lemonade
escapade
persuade
dissuade

### EXTRA WORDS

marinade
comrade
evasive
persuasive
dissuasive

## YEAR 6    LIST 9

concede
precede
recede
impede
stampede
longitude
plenitude
magnitude
solitude
altitude
aptitude
attitude
latitude
gratitude
multitude
fortitude
servitude
intrude

### EXTRA WORDS

secede
centipede
millipede
allude
delude

## YEAR 6    LIST 10

legend
depend
suspend
contend
ascend
descend
transcend
comprehend
recommend
license
incense
condense
defense
offense
immense
expense
intense
pretense

### EXTRA WORDS

stipend
dividend
apprehend
reverend
condescend

## YEAR 6    LIST 11

silence
absence
essence
sentence
difference
audience
patience
obedience
convenience
experience
gradient
lenient
sentient
nutrient
efficient
sufficient
ingredient
resilient

## YEAR 6    LIST 12

guidance
balance
romance
finance
nuisance
distance
instance
entrance
significance
ambulance
sustenance
ambiance
radiance
defiance
reliance
alliance
brilliance
circumstance

## EXTRA WORDS

deficient
proficient
recipient
obedient
convenient

## EXTRA WORDS

radiant
brilliant
significant
financial
circumstantial

## YEAR 6    LIST 13

jealous
zealous
callous
famous
nervous
tremendous
frivolous
fabulous
ridiculous
marvelous
enormous
generous
hideous
gorgeous
courteous
vacuous
conspicuous
ambiguous

## YEAR 6    LIST 14

dubious
gracious
spacious
precious
tedious
various
serious
curious
furious
cautious
devious
previous
obvious
envious
anxious
vivacious
suspicious
hilarious

## EXTRA WORDS

pompous
simultaneous
righteous
arduous
ludicrous

## EXTRA WORDS

variety
curiosity
anxiety
vivacity
hilarity

## YEAR 6    LIST 15

salary
summary
ordinary
stationary
dictionary
library
necessary
military
grocery
surgery
gallery
stationery
cemetery
bravery
slavery
injury
treasury
luxury

### EXTRA WORDS

canary
sorcery
mercury
confectionary
haberdashery

## YEAR 6    LIST 16

theory
memory
factory
victory
history
ivory
category
illusory
compulsory
accessory
obligatory
laboratory
dormitory
territory
satisfactory
directory
contradictory
introductory

### EXTRA WORDS

cursory
lavatory
transitory
historical
categorical

## YEAR 6    LIST 17

probable
available
capable
vegetable
edible
legible
terrible
horrible
sensible
possible
miracle
obstacle
spectacle
icicle
vehicle
article
particle
cuticle

### EXTRA WORDS

enable
liable
eligible
manacle
tentacle

## YEAR 6    LIST 18

criminal
terminal
eternal
principal
mineral
funeral
cathedral
integral
enamel
caramel
colonel
sentinel
carousel
shrivel
satchel
stencil
daffodil
utensil

### EXTRA WORDS

radical
scalpel
snorkel
mongrel
minstrel

## YEAR 6    LIST 19

dual
gradual
manual
annual
casual
visual
usual
ritual
virtual
actual
factual
textual
punctual
residual
individual
perpetual
spiritual
eventual

## YEAR 6    LIST 20

yak
kayak
trek
lilac
maniac
zodiac
havoc
combat
acrobat
format
diplomat
habitat
aristocrat
apricot
despot
chariot
patriot
mascot

### EXTRA WORDS

bilingual
biannual
habitual
intellectual
conceptual

### EXTRA WORDS

anorak
tarmac
wombat
ziggurat
zealot

## YEAR 6    LIST 21

- climax
- convex
- reflex
- complex
- perplex
- prefix
- suffix
- matrix
- hijack
- gimmick
- limerick
- paddock
- hammock
- distinct
- extinct
- instinct
- prompt
- tempt

## YEAR 6    LIST 22

- abrupt
- abstain
- absurd
- adjacent
- advantage
- adversity
- advertise
- analyze
- anatomy
- anecdote
- anoint
- anomaly
- anonymity
- antenna
- anthem
- anticipate
- antidote
- antiseptic

## EXTRA WORDS

- vortex
- ransack
- tussock
- maverick
- precinct

## EXTRA WORDS

- abdicate
- admonish
- advantageous
- anomalous
- anonymous

## YEAR 6   LIST 23

befriend
behalf
behave
benefit
beware
bewilder
decrease
depict
deposit
desert
dessert
despise
despite
detergent
deterrent
develop
deviate
devour

## YEAR 6   LIST 24

compartment
compassion
competent
complaint
compliment
concise
confidence
conflict
congeal
conscience
construct
contempt
context
contrary
contribute
convention
convince
controversy

### EXTRA WORDS

bereaved
demise
depiction
desertion
deviation

### EXTRA WORDS

communal
construe
contaminate
contraption
conservation

## YEAR 6    LIST 25

diary
diagonal
diamond
diameter
dilemma
dilute
diverge
divide
divorce
disaster
discreet
discriminate
disdain
dispatch
disturbance
disarray
disorientated
dissent

## YEAR 6    LIST 26

eclipse
erase
escape
evolve
embark
embody
embroil
enchant
enclose
encounter
enforce
engage
enrage
enroll
envelope
encourage
enthusiasm
enterprise

## EXTRA WORDS

dilate
disappoint
disinfect
disintegrate
dissipate

## EXTRA WORDS

elude
entwine
enumerate
embalm
embroider

## YEAR 6    LIST 27

example
excess
exempt
exotic
expand
expire
explain
explode
exploit
extreme
examine
exception
exclusive
excursion
exemplary
exertion
existence
exhibition

### EXTRA WORDS

extol
exemplify
exterminate
extraordinary
extravagant

## YEAR 6    LIST 28

forfeit
forlorn
forsake
forecast
forehead
foretell
foreboding
oblige
oblong
obscene
observe
obtuse
obstinate
objection
obligation
obstruction
overbearing
overblown

### EXTRA WORDS

forebear
oblivious
obnoxious
obsessive
obtrusive

## YEAR 6    LIST 29

impulse
impediment
imperative
improvise
impudent
inflict
influence
influx
injure
intercept
interfere
intermediate
interrupt
interval
intervene
interview
introduce
introspect

### EXTRA WORDS

incur
influenza
intimidate
introverted
impinge

## YEAR 6    LIST 30

parachute
paradox
paragraph
parallel
paraphrase
parasite
percentage
persistent
pre-exist
prehistoric
prescribe
pretext
proceed
profound
prohibit
proportion
proposal
province

### EXTRA WORDS

parable
precipitous
precursor
pre-empt
procedure

## YEAR 6    LIST 31

recline
recollect
recreation
refrain
regulate
rehearse
relapse
release
remember
remorse
repetition
reproach
repugnant
repulse
resemble
resolve
responsible
restrict

## YEAR 6    LIST 32

rebuke
receipt
recess
re-enact
re-evaluate
rejoice
rejuvenate
retaliate
retort
retreat
retribution
reunion
revelation
revenge
reverse
revive
revolution
revolve

## EXTRA WORDS

rebut
recluse
recur
redeem
remiss

## EXTRA WORDS

reinforce
reimburse
reincarnation
resuscitation
retrospective

## YEAR 6     LIST 33

subjective
sublime
submarine
submit
subscribe
subside
substance
substitute
suburb
superficial
superstition
supervise
supplement
supreme
surname
surpass
survey
survive

## YEAR 6     LIST 34

transfer
transfix
transform
transition
translate
transmit
transparent
transpire
transplant
transport
undermine
underneath
understand
uniform
unison
unity
universe
university

### EXTRA WORDS

subconscious
subordinate
supersede
surfeit
susceptible

### EXTRA WORDS

transience
transaction
transmission
undergrowth
undertaking

## YEAR 6　　LIST 35

accommodate
accurate
affection
apparent
commercial
committee
commotion
communication
community
commute
immediate
immerse
opponent
opportunity
succeed
succinct
surrender
unnecessary

## YEAR 6　　LIST 36

dais
nemesis
genesis
antithesis
hypothesis
synthesis
neurosis
diagnosis
hypnosis
analysis
paralysis
synopsis
stimulus
octopus
apparatus
nucleus
radius
genius

## EXTRA WORDS

appraise
eccentric
oppress
succumb
supplant

## EXTRA WORDS

parenthesis
analyses
syntheses
nuclei
radii

## YEAR 6     LIST 37

diagram
kilogram
program
axiom
idiom
capsicum
referendum
maximum
minimum
pendulum
museum
stadium
medium
premium
aquarium
emporium
gymnasium
vacuum

## YEAR 6     LIST 38

legion
region
religion
battalion
pavilion
stallion
medallion
rebellion
onion
union
companion
opinion
dominion
scorpion
champion
cushion
fashion
criterion

## EXTRA WORDS

madam
milligram
anagram
asylum
curriculum

## EXTRA WORDS

coercion
suspicion
accordion
communion
centurion

## YEAR 6    LIST 39

mansion
pension
tension
evasion
invasion
occasion
persuasion
collision
division
provision
television
confusion
conclusion
illusion
expansion
dimension
extension
diversion

## YEAR 6    LIST 40

option
relation
duration
situation
education
destination
generation
preparation
admiration
tuition
intuition
condition
definition
nutrition
introduction
adoption
perception
description

## EXTRA WORDS

adhesion
cohesion
erosion
explosion
conversion

## EXTRA WORDS

carnation
proclamation
vaccination
composition
prescription

## YEAR 6    LIST 41

passion
session
aggression
expression
impression
oppression
mission
admission
omission
permission
concussion
discussion
percussion
magician
musician
physician
optician
politician

### EXTRA WORDS

succession
obsession
repercussion
beautician
technician

## YEAR 6    LIST 42

obscure
procure
secure
manure
fissure
torture
nurture
structure
scripture
miniature
signature
temperature
literature
furniture
manufacture
architecture
agriculture
adventure

### EXTRA WORDS

conjure
security
obscurity
structural
agricultural

## YEAR 6    LIST 43

sabre
acre
ogre
genre
macabre
massacre
mediocre
theatre
sincere
severe
atmosphere
hemisphere
persevere
veneer
career
pioneer
volunteer
reindeer

## YEAR 6    LIST 44

lament
cement
moment
garment
ferment
torment
fragment
pigment
augment
ailment
equipment
ornament
parliament
vehement
implement
experiment
argument
instrument

## EXTRA WORDS

buccaneer
engineer
revere
severity
sincerity

## EXTRA WORDS

appointment
assignment
environment
ornamental
instrumental

## YEAR 6    LIST 45

incubate
suffocate
confiscate
communicate
congregate
investigate
interrogate
stipulate
congratulate
intimate
evaporate
meditate
amputate
devastate
cultivate
integrate
concentrate
magistrate

## YEAR 6    LIST 46

candidate
circulate
eliminate
assassinate
hibernate
liberate
deliberate
reverberate
refrigerate
exaggerate
accelerate
cooperate
appreciate
associate
appropriate
abbreviate
evacuate
contemplate

### EXTRA WORDS

investigation
evaporation
meditation
devastation
concentration

### EXTRA WORDS

ventilate
gesticulate
procrastinate
exasperate
excavate

## YEAR 6   LIST 47

pious
vicious
luscious
delicious
facetious
atrocious
ferocious
conscious
contagious
religious
ingenious
delirious
glorious
notorious
ambitious
fictitious
infectious
pretentious

### EXTRA WORDS

audacious
fallacious
luxurious
mysterious
victorious

## YEAR 6   LIST 48

vandalism
organism
altruism
magnetism
skepticism
theist
atheist
idealist
florist
dentist
scientist
optimist
pessimist
journalist
capitalist
pragmatist
psychologist
environmentalist

### EXTRA WORDS

materialism
conservatism
monarchist
idealistically
optimistically

## YEAR 6     LIST 49

fete
decor
debris
facade
cuisine
recipe
encore
elite
sabotage
souvenir
amateur
chauffeur
ballet
gourmet
banquet
bouquet
silhouette
restaurant

### EXTRA WORDS

crepe
mousse
gateau
omelet
croissant

## YEAR 6     LIST 50

bias
alias
replica
gondola
opera
stanza
nostalgia
alibi
confetti
bravo
fiasco
soprano
incognito
scenario
quorum
memorandum
millennium
propaganda

### EXTRA WORDS

lasagna
salami
macaroni
spaghetti
gelato

# YEAR 6    REVISION LIST

| | | |
|---|---|---|
| wizard | sacrifice | adhesive |
| routine | persuade | comprehend |
| ascend | obedience | difference |
| patience | peculiar | enormous |
| brilliance | nuisance | anxious |
| compulsory | mediocre | hypothesis |
| ridiculous | spectacle | compliment |
| feminine | cathedral | habitat |
| perplex | distinct | cowardice |
| maniac | advertise | anticipate |
| benefit | contrary | calendar |
| despite | attitude | conscience |
| diamond | extreme | exhibit |
| generous | individual | destination |
| opportunity | alternative | nervous |
| obligation | interview | adventure |
| parachute | premium | revelation |
| substitute | transition | underneath |
| excess | concentrate | available |
| community | encourage | reward |
| nucleus | repetition | synopsis |
| distance | vacuum | ambitious |
| magazine | pavilion | solitude |
| satisfactory | refrigerate | opponent |
| disaster | dimension | occasion |
| confiscate | pessimist | intuition |
| discussion | politician | evacuate |
| structure | surpass | literature |
| volunteer | emporium | atmosphere |
| vehement | companion | serious |
| instrument | preparation | appropriate |
| parliament | suffocate | sincere |
| altruism | recipe | nostalgia |
| | cuisine | |

Made in the USA
Middletown, DE
22 August 2024

59566406R00099